Office 365 Powerpoint for Beginners

Bleu Kaleidoscope, LLC

1. **How to create a new PowerPoint presentation from scratch:**
   - Open PowerPoint from your Office 365 apps.
   - Click on "Blank Presentation" or choose a template to start.

2. **How to add slides and choose different slide layouts:**
   - Click on the "Home" tab.
   - Click the "New Slide" button to add a slide.
   - Choose a slide layout from the gallery.

3. **How to insert text and format it within a slide:**
   - Click on the slide where you want to add text.
   - Start typing or paste text from another source.
   - Highlight the text, then use the "Font" and "Paragraph" sections on the "Home" tab to format it.

4. **How to insert and format images and shapes on a slide:**
   - Click on the slide where you want to add an image or shape.
   - Click the "Insert" tab.
   - Choose "Pictures" to insert an image or "Shapes" to add a shape.
   - Select the image or shape and use the "Format" tab to customize its appearance.

5. **How to apply themes and change the overall design of your presentation:**
   - Click on the "Design" tab.
   - Browse through the available themes and click on one to apply it to your presentation.

6. **How to add animations and transitions between slides:**
   - Click on the slide you want to animate.
   - Go to the "Animations" tab.
   - Choose an animation effect and set its options.
   - To add transitions between slides, go to the "Transitions" tab and select a transition effect.

7. **How to create and customize charts and graphs in PowerPoint:**
   - Click on the "Insert" tab.

* Choose "Chart" or "SmartArt" to create a chart or graph.
* Enter your data and customize the chart as needed using the "Chart Design" and "Format" tabs.

8. How to use the "Presenter View" during a presentation:
* Connect your computer to a projector or second screen.
* Click on the "Slide Show" tab.
* lick "Presenter View" to start your presentation with additional presenter tools.

9. How to record and add narration to your slides:
* Click on the "Slide Show" tab.
* Click "Record Slide Show" and follow the instructions to record narration.

10. How to add video and audio to your presentation:
* Click on the "Insert" tab.
* Choose "Video" or "Audio" to add media files from your computer or online sources.

11. How to insert and edit hyperlinks within your slides:
* Select the text or object you want to hyperlink.
* Click the "Insert" tab.
* Choose "Hyperlink" and enter the link address.

12. How to collaborate with others on a PowerPoint presentation using Office 365's co-authoring features:
* Save your presentation to OneDrive or SharePoint.
* Share the presentation with collaborators and grant them editing permissions.

13. How to use the "Design Ideas" feature to enhance your slides:
* Click on the "Design" tab.
* Click "Design Ideas" to get layout suggestions based on your slide content.

14. How to create custom slide layouts and master slides:
* Go to the "View" tab.

- Click "Slide Master."
- Customize the slide master, which will affect all slides based on that master.

15. How to use the "Slide Show" mode and customize its settings:
- Click on the "Slide Show" tab.
- Click "From Beginning" to start the presentation.
- Use the "Set Up Slide Show" option to customize presentation settings.

16. How to set up and use Presenter Coach to improve your presentation skills:
- Click on the "Rehearse with Coach" option in the "Slide Show" tab.
- Follow the prompts to rehearse your presentation while receiving feedback.

17. How to add and customize SmartArt graphics:
- Click on the "Insert" tab.
- Choose "SmartArt" and select a graphic type.
- Enter your content and customize the SmartArt using the "SmartArt Design" and "Format" tabs.

18. How to use the "Morph" transition for seamless animations between slides:
- Ensure you have at least two slides with similar objects.
- Go to the "Transitions" tab.
- Choose "Morph" as the transition for the second slide.

19. How to export your presentation to PDF or other formats:
- Click on the "File" tab.
- Choose "Export" and then select the desired format (e.g., PDF, PPTX).

20. How to add and format tables in PowerPoint:
- Click on the "Insert" tab.
- Choose "Table" and select the desired number of rows and columns.

- Use the "Table Design" and "Table Layout" tabs to format the table.

21. How to use the "Ink to Text" and "Ink to Shape" features with a stylus or touch-enabled device:

- Click on the "Draw" tab.
- Use a stylus or your finger to draw shapes or write text.
- PowerPoint will automatically convert your handwriting into shapes or text.

22. How to set up and use PowerPoint's "Slide Zoom" feature for interactive presentations:

- Click on the "Insert" tab.
- Choose "Zoom" and select "Slide Zoom" to add a zoomed-in view of a specific slide.

23. How to protect your PowerPoint presentation with a password:

- Click on the "File" tab.
- Choose "Protect Presentation" and then "Encrypt with Password."
- Enter a password to protect the file.

24. How to use the "Tell Me" feature to quickly find commands and options:

- Click on the "Tell Me" box located on the Ribbon.
- Type the action or feature you want to find, and PowerPoint will provide relevant suggestions.

25. How to integrate PowerPoint with other Office 365 apps like Word and Excel:

- Use the "Insert" tab to add objects, tables, or charts from other Office apps.
- Save your PowerPoint presentation to OneDrive or SharePoint to enable seamless collaboration with other Office apps.

26. How to create a custom PowerPoint template for consistent branding:

- Design your slides with the desired layout, colors, fonts, and branding elements.
- Go to the "File" tab, choose "Save As," and select "PowerPoint Template (*.potx)" as the file format.

27. How to use PowerPoint Designer to automatically create professional-looking slides:
- Click on the "Design" tab.
- Click "Design Ideas" to let PowerPoint suggest slide layouts based on your content.

28. How to insert 3D models and icons into your presentation:
- Click on the "Insert" tab.
- Choose "3D Models" to add 3D objects or "Icons" to insert vector icons.

29. How to add and format equations using PowerPoint's built-in equation editor:
- Click on the "Insert" tab.
- Choose "Equation" and select from pre-built equations or build your own.

30. How to create and use slide sections to organize your presentation:
- Go to the "Home" tab.
- Click "Section" to group slides under specific headings.

31. How to use the "Eyedropper" tool to match colors from images or other objects:
- Select the shape or text whose color you want to match.
- Go to the "Format" tab, click "Eyedropper," and then pick a color from the image or object.

32. How to crop and edit images directly within PowerPoint:
- Select the image you want to edit.
- Go to the "Format" tab, click "Crop," and then adjust the cropping handles as needed.

33. How to add and edit audio bookmarks for precise audio

playback during the presentation:
- Click on the "Audio" icon in the slide.
- Go to the "Audio Tools Playback" tab and click "Trim Audio."
- Use the bookmarks to set the start and end points of the audio.

34. How to convert a PowerPoint presentation to a video:
- Click on the "File" tab.
- Choose "Export" and then "Create a Video."
- Select the video quality and timings, then click "Create Video."

35. How to use the "Accessibility Checker" to ensure your presentation is accessible to all users:
- Click on the "Review" tab.
- Click "Check Accessibility" to review and fix any potential accessibility issues.

36. How to embed online videos from platforms like YouTube into your presentation:
- Go to the YouTube video you want to embed.
- Click "Share" and then "Embed."
- Copy the embed code and paste it into a PowerPoint slide.

37. How to use the "Gridlines" and "Guides" to align and position objects precisely:
- Go to the "View" tab.
- Check the "Gridlines" and "Guides" options to show them on the slide.

38. How to create interactive navigation using hyperlinked buttons:
- Create shape buttons on your slide.
- Right-click on a shape, select "Hyperlink," and choose the slide or URL you want to link.

39. How to customize the PowerPoint Quick Access Toolbar with frequently used commands:
- Click on the drop-down arrow on the Quick Access Toolbar.
- Choose "More Commands" and then add your preferred commands to the toolbar.

40. How to use "Alt Text" to add descriptive text to images for better accessibility:
- Select the image you want to add Alt Text to.
- Go to the "Format" tab and click "Alt Text."
- Enter a description for the image in the "Description" field.

41. How to embed fonts in your PowerPoint presentation to ensure consistency across devices:
- Go to the "File" tab.
- Choose "Save As," then click "Tools" and select "Save Options."
- Check the "Embed fonts in the file" option and save the presentation.

42. How to recover a previous version of your presentation using version history:
- Go to OneDrive or SharePoint where your presentation is stored.
- Right-click on the file, choose "Version history," and select the version you want to restore.

43. How to use the "Selection Pane" to manage complex slide objects:
- Go to the "Home" tab.
- Click "Select" and choose "Selection Pane."
- Use the pane to show, hide, or reorder objects on the slide.

44. How to create custom slide shows to present selected slides from your presentation:
- Go to the "Slide Show" tab.
- Click "Custom Slide Show" and choose "Custom Shows."
- Create and name your custom slide show with specific slides.

45. How to use PowerPoint QuickStarter to research and outline your presentation topic:
- Click on the "Home" tab.
- Click "QuickStarter" and enter your topic.
- PowerPoint will provide suggested sections and recommended content.

46. How to embed live web content, such as webpages, into your presentation:
- Go to the "Insert" tab.
- Choose "Web Page" and enter the URL to embed a live webpage.

47. How to add and customize icons from the "Icons" library:
- Click on the "Insert" tab.
- Choose "Icons" and search for an icon to insert.
- Resize, recolor, or rotate the icon using the "Format" tab.

48. How to use the "Slide Sorter" view to rearrange slides quickly:
- Go to the "View" tab.
- Click "Slide Sorter" to see a thumbnail view of all slides.
- Drag and drop slides to reorder them.

49. How to create a looping PowerPoint presentation for kiosks or displays:
- Click on the "Slide Show" tab.
- Choose "Set Up Slide Show" and check the "Loop continuously until 'Esc'" option.

50. How to export speaker notes to Word for easy printing or editing:
- Click on the "File" tab.
- Choose "Export" and then "Create Handouts."
- Select "Notes next to slides" and customize the layout as needed.

51. How to use the "Ink Replay" feature to replay your drawings or annotations:
- Click on the "Draw" tab.
- Choose "Ink Replay" and click "Play" to watch the ink strokes being drawn.

52. How to use the "Screen Recording" feature to record your screen and insert it into a slide:

- Click on the "Insert" tab.
- Choose "Screen Recording" and select the area of the screen you want to record.
- Click "Record" to start the screen recording.

53. How to use the "Object Zoom" feature to zoom in on specific objects within a slide:
- Select the object you want to zoom in on.
- Go to the "Insert" tab, click "Zoom," and choose "Object Zoom."

54. How to collaborate on a PowerPoint presentation in real-time using PowerPoint Online:
- Save your presentation to OneDrive or SharePoint.
- Click "Share" and invite collaborators to edit the presentation simultaneously.

55. How to use the "Design Options" to fine-tune the design elements of your slide:
- Click on the "Design" tab.
- Hover over a design option and click the drop-down arrow to access more design variations.

56. How to use the "Insert 3D Models Online" to access 3D models from Microsoft's online library:
- Click on the "Insert" tab.
- Choose "3D Models" and select "From Online Sources."

57. How to use "Alt Text" for images to improve searchability and accessibility:
- Select the image, go to the "Format" tab, click "Alt Text," and add a descriptive alternative text.

58. How to merge shapes to create custom shapes:
- Select the shapes you want to merge.
- Go to the "Format" tab, click "Merge Shapes," and choose the desired merge option.

59. How to use PowerPoint's "Audio Styles" to apply pre-set audio effects:

* Click on the audio icon on the slide.
* Go to the "Audio Tools Playback" tab and choose an audio style from the gallery.

60. How to use the "Recolor" feature to change the color of images and icons:
* Select the image or icon.
* Go to the "Format" tab, click "Color," and choose a new color scheme.

61. How to use the "Format Painter" to apply formatting from one object to another:
* Select the object with the desired formatting.
* Go to the "Home" tab and click "Format Painter."
* Click on the target object to apply the formatting.

62. How to use "Picture Background Removal" to remove the background from an image:
* Select the image.
* Go to the "Format" tab, click "Remove Background," and use the markers to mark areas to keep or remove.

63. How to compress images in a PowerPoint presentation to reduce file size:
* Click on the image.
* Go to the "Format" tab, click "Compress Pictures," and choose a resolution option.

64. How to embed and play online videos without leaving the presentation:
* Go to the "Insert" tab.
* Choose "Video" and select "Online Video."
* Enter the video's URL or search for it on Bing.

65. How to use the "Format Background" feature to change the slide background color or image:
* Go to the "Design" tab.
* Click "Format Background" and choose a color, gradient, texture, or picture.

66. How to use "Slide Zoom" to create summary slides linking to specific sections:
- Go to the "Insert" tab.
- Choose "Zoom" and select "Slide Zoom."
- Add summary content and hyperlink it to other slides.

67. How to save a PowerPoint presentation as a PowerPoint Show (*.ppsx) for easy playback:
- Click on the "File" tab.
- Choose "Save As" and select "PowerPoint Show (*.ppsx)" as the file format.

68. How to enable the "AutoSave" feature in PowerPoint Online to automatically save changes:
- Go to the "File" tab and click "Save As."
- Choose "Browse" and then select your OneDrive or SharePoint location.

69. How to use "Remove Background" to remove unwanted parts from an image:
- Select the image.
- Go to the "Format" tab, click "Remove Background," and adjust the selection as needed.

70. How to use the "Researcher" feature to find and insert reliable information from the web:
- Click on the "Review" tab.
- Choose "Researcher" and enter a search term to find relevant content.

71. How to use PowerPoint's "Slide Show Recording" to record your presentation with timings and narrations:
- Click on the "Slide Show" tab.
- Click "Record Slide Show" and select "Start Recording from Beginning."

72. How to use the "Outline View" to organize and restructure your presentation:

- Click on the "View" tab.
- Choose "Outline View" to view and edit the presentation's text outline.

73. How to use "Merge Shapes" to create custom shapes by combining multiple shapes:
- Select the shapes you want to merge.
- Go to the "Format" tab, click "Merge Shapes," and select the desired merge option.

74. How to use "Presenter View" to view presenter notes and upcoming slides during a presentation:
- Connect your computer to a projector or second screen.
- Click on the "Slide Show" tab and select "Presenter View."

75. How to convert a PowerPoint presentation into a Word document for easy editing and formatting:
- Click on the "File" tab.
- Choose "Save As," then select "Word Document (*.docx)."

76. How to use PowerPoint's "Insert Data from Picture" feature to convert a table from an image into an editable table:
- Click on the "Insert" tab.
- Choose "Table" and then "Insert Data from Picture."
- Take a photo or select an image with the table, and PowerPoint will convert it into an editable table.

77. How to use the "Animation Painter" to copy animations from one object to another:
- Select the animated object with the desired animation.
- Go to the "Animations" tab and click "Animation Painter."
- Click on the target object to apply the animation.

78. How to use the "Eyedropper" tool to pick a color from any element on the slide:
- Go to the "Format" tab.
- Click "Eyedropper" and then click on the color you want to use.

79. How to use the "Slide Show" tab to set up and customize presenter options:

- Go to the "Slide Show" tab.
- Explore options like "Set Up Slide Show," "Rehearse Timings," and "Record Slide Show."

80. How to use the "Alt + Shift + Left/Right Arrow" shortcut to move objects precisely:

- Select the object you want to move.
- Hold "Alt + Shift" on your keyboard and use the arrow keys to move the object in small increments.

81. How to use the "SmartArt" cycle diagrams to illustrate processes or sequences:

- Click on the "Insert" tab.
- Choose "SmartArt" and then "Cycle" to pick a cycle diagram layout.

82. How to use PowerPoint's "Formulas" to perform calculations within tables and text boxes:

- Click on the table cell or text box where you want to insert the formula.
- Enter "=SUM()" or other supported functions and references.

83. How to create a custom animation path for an object on a slide:

- Select the object you want to animate.
- Go to the "Animations" tab and click "Add Animation."
- Choose "Motion Paths" and select a custom path or draw your own with the "Draw Custom Path" option.

84. How to use the "Format Painter" to copy text formatting to multiple text boxes:

- Select the text with the desired formatting.
- Go to the "Home" tab and click "Format Painter."
- Click on the other text boxes to apply the formatting.

85. How to add a drop shadow or reflection to objects in PowerPoint:

- Select the object you want to add a drop shadow or reflection to.
- Go to the "Format" tab, click "Shadow" or "Reflection," and choose the desired style.

86. How to use the "Export to Video" feature to save your presentation as a video file:
- Click on the "File" tab.
- Choose "Export," then select "Create a Video."

87. How to use the "Picture Effects" to apply various artistic effects to images:
- Select the image.
- Go to the "Format" tab, click "Picture Effects," and choose the desired effect category.

88. How to use PowerPoint's "Find and Replace" feature to quickly update text across multiple slides:
- Go to the "Home" tab.
- Click "Replace" in the Editing group and enter the text you want to find and replace.

89. How to use the "Quick Parts" feature to insert pre-built content or reusable elements:
- Go to the "Insert" tab.
- Click "Quick Parts" and choose from "Building Blocks Organizer" or "Document Property" options.

90. How to set up and use presenter notes for reference during your presentation:
- Go to the "View" tab.
- Click "Notes Page" to add and edit notes for each slide.

91. How to use the "Change Case" feature to quickly change the capitalization of text:
- Select the text you want to change.
- Go to the "Home" tab and click "Change Case" to choose the desired capitalization style.

92. How to use the "Rehearse Timings" feature to practice and record slide timings for a self-running presentation:
- Click on the "Slide Show" tab.
- Choose "Rehearse Timings" and follow the on-screen instructions to rehearse your presentation.

93. How to use the "Remove Background" tool to remove a solid-colored background from an image:
- Select the image.
- Go to the "Format" tab, click "Remove Background," and adjust the selection as needed.

94. How to create interactive navigation using hyperlinked objects like images or shapes:
- Select the object you want to hyperlink.
- Go to the "Insert" tab, click "Hyperlink," and choose the slide or URL you want to link.

95. How to use the "Zoom In" and "Zoom Out" features to emphasize specific content during a presentation:
- Go to the "Insert" tab.
- Click "Zoom" and choose "Summary Zoom" or "Slide Zoom" to zoom in or out during the presentation.

96. How to use PowerPoint's "Language Preferences" to set the proofing and display languages:
- Click on the "File" tab.
- Choose "Options," then go to the "Language" section to adjust your language preferences.

97. How to use the "Save As Picture" feature to save a slide or a selection as an image:
- Go to the "File" tab.
- Choose "Save As," then select "PNG" or "JPG" as the file format.

98. How to use the "Embed Fonts" option to ensure font consistency across different devices:
- Click on the "File" tab.

- Choose "Options," go to the "Save" section, and check the "Embed fonts in the file" option.

99. How to use PowerPoint's "Scribble" feature to draw freehand shapes or annotations:
- Go to the "Draw" tab.
- Choose "Scribble" and use your mouse or touchscreen to draw.

100. How to use PowerPoint's "Accessibility Checker" to ensure your presentation meets accessibility standards:
- Click on the "File" tab.
- Choose "Check for Issues," then "Check Accessibility" to review and fix potential accessibility problems.

101. How to use the "Ruler" to precisely align objects on a slide:
- Go to the "View" tab.
- Click "Ruler" to show or hide the horizontal and vertical rulers.

102. How to crop an image to a specific shape using the "Crop to Shape" feature:
- Select the image you want to crop.
- Go to the "Format" tab, click "Crop," and choose the desired shape.

103. How to use "Presenter View" with multiple monitors to see notes, slides, and audience views:
- Connect your computer to multiple monitors.
- Start the slide show, and Presenter View will automatically display on one screen.

104. How to use PowerPoint's "Picture Layouts" to organize multiple pictures on a slide:
- Go to the "Insert" tab.
- Choose "Picture Layout" to select from various picture organization options.

105. How to use the "Merge Formatting" option when pasting content from other sources:

- Copy the content you want to paste into PowerPoint.
- Use "Ctrl + V" to paste the content, then click on the "Paste Options" icon to choose "Merge Formatting."

106. How to use the "Export as PDF" feature to save your presentation as a PDF document:
- Click on the "File" tab.
- Choose "Export" and then "Create PDF/XPS Document."

107. How to create and use custom animations using "Motion Paths":
- Select the object you want to animate.
- Go to the "Animations" tab, click "Add Animation," and choose "More Motion Paths."

108. How to use the "Group" and "Ungroup" features to manipulate multiple objects as one unit or individually:
- Select the objects you want to group.
- Go to the "Format" tab, click "Group," and choose "Group" or "Ungroup."

109. How to use the "Insert Equation" feature to add mathematical equations and symbols:
- Click on the "Insert" tab.
- Choose "Equation" and select "Insert New Equation."

110. How to use PowerPoint's "Designer" feature to create stunning design variations for your slides:
- Click on the "Design" tab.
- PowerPoint Designer will automatically offer design suggestions based on your slide content.

111. How to use the "Object Rotation" feature to rotate objects at custom angles:
- Select the object you want to rotate.
- Go to the "Format" tab, click "Rotate," and choose the desired rotation angle.

112. How to use PowerPoint's "Accessibility Checker" to review

and improve accessibility issues in your presentation:

- Click on the "Review" tab.
- Choose "Check Accessibility" to run the accessibility checker.

113. How to use the "Speaker Notes" section to add detailed notes for each slide:

- Go to the "View" tab.
- Click "Notes Page" to see the slide with its associated notes.

114. How to create custom animations with "Trigger" animations to start an effect based on a specific action:

- Go to the "Animations" tab.
- Click "Add Animation," then choose the desired animation.
- Click "Animation Pane," select the animation, and click "Add Trigger."

115. How to use the "Selection Pane" to manage complex slide objects and layers:

- Go to the "Home" tab.
- Click "Select," then choose "Selection Pane."

116. How to use the "Zoom for PowerPoint" add-in to enhance interactive presentations:

- Install the "Zoom for PowerPoint" add-in from the Microsoft AppSource.
- Use it to create and manage zooming effects and navigation links.

117. How to use "File Versioning" in OneDrive or SharePoint to access previous versions of your presentation:

- Go to the "File" tab and click "Version History" to see and restore previous versions.

118. How to add a custom watermark or logo to your slides for branding purposes:

- Go to the "Insert" tab.
- Choose "Header & Footer" and then "Slide" to add a watermark or logo.

119. How to use the "Online Pictures" feature to search and insert images from various online sources:
- Click on the "Insert" tab.
- Choose "Online Pictures" and use the search box to find images

120. How to use PowerPoint's "Outline View" to rearrange and organize slide content quickly:
- Go to the "View" tab.
- Click "Outline View" to work with the presentation's text outline.

121. How to use the "Image Background Removal" tool to remove the background from images:
- Click on the image.
- Go to the "Format" tab, click "Remove Background," and use the markers to mark areas to keep or remove.

122. How to use "Animation Pane" to manage and customize animations for individual slide elements:
- Go to the "Animations" tab.
- Click "Animation Pane" to open the Animation Pane and view/manage all animations.

123. How to use the "Slide Master" to apply consistent formatting across all slides in your presentation:
- Go to the "View" tab.
- Click "Slide Master" to access and customize the slide master and layout master slides.

124. How to use "Action Buttons" to create interactive navigation elements within your presentation:
- Go to the "Insert" tab.
- Choose "Action" and select a pre-built action button or draw your own custom action button.

125. How to use PowerPoint's "Quick Analysis" feature to create charts and graphs from data in your presentation:
- Select the data you want to visualize.

- Click on the "Quick Analysis" icon that appears, and then
  choose the desired chart type.

126. How to use the "Presenter Coach" feature to practice and receive feedback on your presentation delivery:
- Go to the "Slide Show" tab.
- Click "Rehearse with Coach" to start the Presenter Coach
  feature.

127. How to use PowerPoint's "Eyedropper" to match the color of an object to any element on your slide:
- Go to the "Format" tab.
- Click "Eyedropper" and then click on the color you want to
  match.

128. How to create custom slide show timings for each slide in your presentation:
- Go to the "Transitions" tab.
- Check the "After" box and enter the desired time for each slide.

129. How to use the "Office Timeline" add-in to create professional timelines and Gantt charts:
- Install the "Office Timeline" add-in from the Microsoft
  AppSource.
- Use it to build timelines directly within PowerPoint.

130. How to use the "Slide Show Recording" feature to record your presentation with narration and slide timings:
- Click on the "Slide Show" tab.
- Choose "Record Slide Show" and select "Start Recording from
  Beginning."

131. How to use PowerPoint's "Send to OneNote" feature to send your presentation slides to a OneNote notebook:
- Go to the "File" tab.
- Choose "Send to OneNote" and select the desired notebook
  section.

132. How to use the "Slide Number" feature to add slide numbers to your presentation:
- Go to the "Insert" tab.
- Choose "Slide Number" and select the desired location for the slide numbers.

133. How to use the "Slide Show" tab to set up and customize slide show options:
- Go to the "Slide Show" tab.
- Explore options like "Set Up Show," "Rehearse Timings," and "Presenter View."

134. How to use the "Alt Text" option for charts and SmartArt graphics to enhance accessibility:
- Right-click on the chart or SmartArt.
- Choose "Edit Alt Text" and enter a description for accessibility.

135. How to use PowerPoint's "Convert to Shape" feature to convert text to editable shapes:
- Select the text you want to convert.
- Go to the "Format" tab, click "Convert to Shape," and choose the desired shape.

136. How to use the "Play in Background" feature to insert audio that plays across multiple slides:
- Go to the "Insert" tab.
- Choose "Audio" and then "Play in Background."

137. How to use the "Crop to Fill" option to resize images while preserving the aspect ratio:
- Select the image you want to resize.
- Go to the "Format" tab, click "Crop," and choose "Crop to Fill."

138. How to use the "Zoom for PowerPoint" add-in to create interactive navigation links and sections:
- Install the "Zoom for PowerPoint" add-in from the Microsoft AppSource.
- Use it to create zoomable sections within your presentation.

139. How to use PowerPoint's "Chart Elements" feature to add or remove chart elements:
- Click on the chart.
- Go to the "Chart Design" tab and click "Add Chart Element."

140. How to use PowerPoint's "Record Audio" feature to add narration to your slides:
- Go to the "Insert" tab.
- Choose "Audio" and then "Record Audio" to record your narration.

141. How to use "Smart Lookup" to quickly access definitions, explanations, and related information:
- Right-click on a word or phrase.
- Choose "Smart Lookup" to open the Insights pane.

142. How to use the "Embed Fonts" option to ensure font consistency when sharing your presentation:
- Click on the "File" tab.
- Choose "Options," go to the "Save" section, and check the "Embed fonts in the file" option.

143. How to use PowerPoint's "Line Spacing" feature to adjust the space between lines of text:
- Select the text you want to modify.
- Go to the "Home" tab, click the "Line Spacing" icon, and choose the desired spacing.

144. How to use the "Arrange" feature to change the order of overlapping objects on a slide:
- Select the objects you want to rearrange.
- Go to the "Format" tab, click "Arrange," and choose "Bring to Front" or "Send to Back."

145. How to use PowerPoint's "Morph Transition" to create smooth animations between slides with similar objects:
- Ensure you have at least two slides with similar objects.
- Go to the "Transitions" tab, select "Morph" as the transition for the second slide.

146. How to use the "Animation Painter" to copy animations from one object to multiple objects:
- Select the object with the desired animation.
- Go to the "Animations" tab and click "Animation Painter."
- Click on each object to apply the animation.

147. How to use "Presenter Coach" to receive feedback on pacing, language, and inclusivity in your presentation:
- Go to the "Slide Show" tab.
- Click "Rehearse with Coach" to start the Presenter Coach feature.

148. How to use "Office Intelligent Services" to get design recommendations and generate slide content:
- Click on the "Design" tab.
- Explore "Design Ideas" for suggested layouts and content.

149. How to use the "Presenter View" with a single monitor to view notes and slides privately:
- Go to the "Slide Show" tab.
- Click "Presenter View" to start the presentation in Presenter View mode.

150. How to use "Slide Master" to create consistent background and formatting for all slides:
- Go to the "View" tab.
- Click "Slide Master" to access the slide master and apply changes to all slides.

151. How to use "Guides" to align and position objects precisely on the slide:
- Go to the "View" tab.
- Click "Guides" to show or hide horizontal and vertical guides on the slide.

152. How to use PowerPoint's "Slide Zoom" to create hyperlinks to specific slides within your presentation:
- Select the object (e.g., a shape) you want to use as the link.
- Go to the "Insert" tab, click "Zoom," and choose "Slide Zoom."

- Select the slide you want to link to.

153. How to use the "Accessibility Checker" to ensure your presentation meets accessibility guidelines:
- Click on the "Review" tab.
- Choose "Check Accessibility" to review and address any accessibility issues.

154. How to use PowerPoint's "Image Transparency" feature to make images partially see-through:
- Select the image you want to adjust.
- Go to the "Format" tab, click "Transparency," and adjust the transparency slider.

155. How to use the "Recording Timer" to keep track of the duration while recording your presentation:
- Click on the "Slide Show" tab.
- Click "Start Recording" and the recording timer will appear on the bottom-left corner.

156. How to use the "Merge Shapes" feature to combine multiple shapes into one:
- Select the shapes you want to merge.
- Go to the "Format" tab, click "Merge Shapes," and choose the desired merge option.

157. How to use "Slide Master" to set a consistent font style for all slide titles and text:
- Go to the "View" tab.
- Click "Slide Master," select the title and text placeholders, and apply the desired font style.

158. How to use the "Picture Color" feature to apply various color effects to images:
- Select the image you want to modify.
- Go to the "Format" tab, click "Color," and choose the desired color effect.

159. How to use the "Designer" feature to create design ideas for your slides:
- Click on the "Design" tab.
- PowerPoint Designer will automatically offer design suggestions based on your slide content.

160. How to use "Slide Sorter" view to rearrange and manage slides quickly:
- Go to the "View" tab.
- Click "Slide Sorter" to view and manage all slides as thumbnails.

161. How to use PowerPoint's "Collapse" and "Expand" sections to organize content in the Outline view:
- Go to the "View" tab.
- Click "Outline View," and use the "+" and "-" icons to collapse and expand sections.

162. How to use "Alt Text" for shapes and SmartArt to enhance accessibility:
- Right-click on the shape or SmartArt.
- Choose "Edit Alt Text" and add a description for accessibility.

163. How to use the "Animation Painter" to copy animations from one object to multiple objects:
- Select the object with the desired animation.
- Go to the "Animations" tab, click "Animation Painter," and click on other objects to apply the animation.

164. How to use "PowerPoint for Android/iOS" to create, edit, and present presentations on mobile devices:
- Download the PowerPoint app from your device's app store.
- Sign in with your Microsoft account to access your presentations.

165. How to use "PowerPoint Online" to collaborate on presentations in a web browser:
- Go to the Microsoft Office website (office.com) and sign in with your Microsoft account.

- Click "PowerPoint" to create or open a presentation and collaborate with others in real-time.

166. How to use the "Split" option to divide a text box into multiple columns:
- Click on the text box.
- Go to the "Format" tab, click "Text Box," and choose the number of columns.

167. How to use the "Outline View" to easily edit and reorganize slide content:
- Go to the "View" tab.
- Click "Outline View" to see and edit the text outline of your presentation.

168. How to use PowerPoint's "Quick Access Toolbar" to add frequently used commands for easy access:
- Click on the drop-down arrow on the Quick Access Toolbar.
- Choose "More Commands" and add your preferred commands to the toolbar.

169. How to use "Comments" to collaborate and leave feedback on specific parts of a presentation:
- Go to the "Review" tab.
- Click "New Comment," and enter your comment in the speech bubble that appears.

170. How to use "Alt Text" for charts to provide a description for visually impaired users:
- Right-click on the chart.
- Choose "Edit Alt Text" and add a description for accessibility.

171. How to use PowerPoint's "Animation Pane" to manage and customize animations for individual slide elements:
- Go to the "Animations" tab.
- Click "Animation Pane" to open the Animation Pane and view/ manage all animations.

172. How to use the "Slide Show" tab to set up and customize presenter options:
- Go to the "Slide Show" tab.
- Explore options like "Set Up Slide Show," "Rehearse Timings," and "Record Slide Show."

173. How to use the "Selection Pane" to manage complex slide objects and layers:
- Go to the "Home" tab.
- Click "Select," then choose "Selection Pane."

174. How to use "Office Intelligent Services" to get design recommendations and generate slide content:
- Click on the "Design" tab.
- Explore "Design Ideas" for suggested layouts and content.

175. How to use the "Presenter View" with a single monitor to view notes and slides privately:
- Go to the "Slide Show" tab.
- Click "Presenter View" to start the presentation in Presenter View mode.

176. How to use "Merge Shapes" to create custom shapes by combining multiple shapes:
- Select the shapes you want to merge.
- Go to the "Format" tab, click "Merge Shapes," and select the desired merge option.

177. How to use PowerPoint's "Action Buttons" to create interactive navigation elements:
- Go to the "Insert" tab.
- Choose "Shapes" and select an action button from the "Action Buttons" group.

178. How to use the "Notes Master" to add headers, footers, and logos to presenter notes:
- Go to the "View" tab.
- Click "Notes Master" to customize the notes layout.

179. How to use the "Picture Border" feature to add borders and frames to images:
- Select the image you want to modify.
- Go to the "Format" tab, click "Picture Border," and choose the desired border style.

180. How to use PowerPoint's "Presenter View" to deliver a presentation with speaker notes and slide thumbnails:
- Connect your computer to a second screen or projector.
- Start the slide show, and Presenter View will automatically appear on the second screen.

181. How to use "Slide Master" to set up a consistent background for all slides:
- Go to the "View" tab.
- Click "Slide Master," select the slide master, and customize the background.

182. How to use the "Format Painter" to copy formatting from one object to another:
- Select the object with the desired formatting.
- Go to the "Home" tab and click "Format Painter."
- Click on the target object to apply the formatting.

183. How to use "Alt Text" for tables to provide accessible descriptions for screen readers:
- Right-click on the table.
- Choose "Edit Alt Text" and add a description for accessibility.

184. How to use PowerPoint's "Slide Show" tab to set up advanced slide show options:
- Go to the "Slide Show" tab.
- Explore options like "Set Up Show," "Rehearse Timings," and "Presenter View."

185. How to use "SmartArt" to create and customize professional graphics and diagrams:
- Go to the "Insert" tab.

- Choose "SmartArt," select a category, and pick a SmartArt graphic.

186. How to use "Section Headers" to organize slides into sections in the Slide Sorter view:
- Go to the "View" tab.
- Click "Slide Sorter," right-click on a slide, and choose "Add Section."

187. How to use the "Selection Pane" to manage complex slide objects and layers:
- Go to the "Home" tab.
- Click "Select," then choose "Selection Pane."

188. How to use "Alt Text" for shapes to provide a description for visually impaired users:
- Right-click on the shape.
- Choose "Edit Alt Text" and add a description for accessibility.

189. How to use the "Developer" tab to add interactive form controls to your presentation:
- Go to the "File" tab and choose "Options."
- In the PowerPoint Options dialog, click "Customize Ribbon," and enable the "Developer" tab.

190. How to use "Alt Text" for embedded videos to enhance accessibility:
- Right-click on the video.
- Choose "Edit Alt Text" and add a description for accessibility.

191. How to use PowerPoint's "Line Spacing" feature to adjust the space between lines of text:
- Select the text you want to modify.
- Go to the "Home" tab, click the "Line Spacing" icon, and choose the desired spacing.

192. How to use "Alt Text" for shapes and SmartArt to enhance accessibility:
- Right-click on the shape or SmartArt.

• Choose "Edit Alt Text" and add a description for accessibility.

193. How to use the "Animation Painter" to copy animations from one object to multiple objects:
• Select the object with the desired animation.
• Go to the "Animations" tab, click "Animation Painter," and click on other objects to apply the animation.

194. How to use "PowerPoint for Android/iOS" to create, edit, and present presentations on mobile devices:
• Download the PowerPoint app from your device's app store.
• Sign in with your Microsoft account to access your presentations.

195. How to use "PowerPoint Online" to collaborate on presentations in a web browser:
• Go to the Microsoft Office website (office.com) and sign in with your Microsoft account.
• Click "PowerPoint" to create or open a presentation and collaborate with others in real-time.

196. How to use the "Split" option to divide a text box into multiple columns:
• Click on the text box.
• Go to the "Format" tab, click "Text Box," and choose the number of columns.

197. How to use "Comments" to collaborate and leave feedback on specific parts of a presentation:
• Go to the "Review" tab.
• Click "New Comment," and enter your comment in the speech bubble that appears.

198. How to use "Alt Text" for charts to provide a description for visually impaired users:
• Right-click on the chart.
• Choose "Edit Alt Text" and add a description for accessibility.

199. How to use PowerPoint's "Animation Pane" to manage and customize animations for individual slide elements:
- Go to the "Animations" tab.
- Click "Animation Pane" to open the Animation Pane and view/ manage all animations.

200. How to use the "Slide Show" tab to set up and customize presenter options:
- Go to the "Slide Show" tab.
- Explore options like "Set Up Slide Show," "Rehearse Timings," and "Record Slide Show."